I l … sh

Roger Stev … rtist who is now ma … hildren's poet and p … visits schools, festivals, museums and libraries all over the country, bringing music, humour and lots of audience participation to his performances. He has published several children's novels and his poems appear regularly in anthologies. This is his first solo collection.

Roger's award-winning web site, The Poetry Zone, was set up in 1998. You can visit it on http://www.poetryzone.co.uk

While not preoccupied with the disturbances caused by the West London Panda Posse, Jane Eccles divides her time between her career as a secret agent and her passion for illustrating Martian joke books. In the real world, she also illustrates books for earthlings.

I Did Not Eat the Goldfish

Poems by Roger Stevens

Illustrated by Jane Eccles

MACMILLAN CHILDREN'S BOOKS

For Lily

First published 2002
by Macmillan Children's Books
a division of Macmillan Publishers Ltd
20 New Wharf Road, London N1 9RR
Basingstoke and Oxford
www.panmacmillan.com

Associated companies throughout the world

ISBN 0 330 39718 4

1 3 5 7 9 8 6 4 2

A CIP catalogue record for this book is available from the British Library.

Printed and bound in the UK by CPI Mackays, Chatham ME5 8TD

Contents

Poem for Sale

Poem for sale
(One careful owner)
With simile,
(As lucky as a dime)
Two exquisite
And erudite adjectives
And one rhyme
Going
For a song

Spell For My Father

Oh,
But if there was a spell
To bring my father back
I would gather its components at once.
His watch, still ticking,
His old, grey, baggy jumper
A photograph of his smile
A compass and a candle.

I would whisper the spell late into the night
I would say it loud, shout it, sing it
The whole world and his neighbour
Would hear me singing.

Ah,
But there is no spell
To bring him back.
Only the sun rising in the East
And a prayer
For a new beginning.

Father Christmas

Dear Father Christmas
Please bring me someone –
with a funny grin
that lets love in,
with a tender kiss
that makes me shiver
and feel warm inside,
with lovely brown
cockerspaniel eyes,
with magic in her fingertips
like Paul Daniels
and riddles and jokes
and games,

with a world of love
to share.

Dear Father Christmas,
Please bring Dad someone
too.

Lighthouse

I wanted to go up the lighthouse
on Plymouth Ho.
It was a great tall building
solid and dark against the windy sky.

I can't take you, Mum said,
on account of my claustrophobia.
All those steps; it's too enclosed,
No windows until you reach the top.

I can't take you, Dad said,
on account of my vertigo;
I shall get dizzy and want to jump off.

So they asked a stranger to take me.

We climbed and climbed
until there I stood,
surveying a vast silvery sea,
where the whole world
stretched before me
In a dazzling eternity of colour.

And below me
Mum and Dad
huddled earthbound
like ants, trapped
in a fear they had grown
like the weeds
tangled around the beans
in Dad's garden.

Food for Thought

If every star
In this galaxy
Were a grain of salt
It would fill
An Olympic-sized
Swimming pool

And if you filled
That pool with water
It would be
Very, very salty

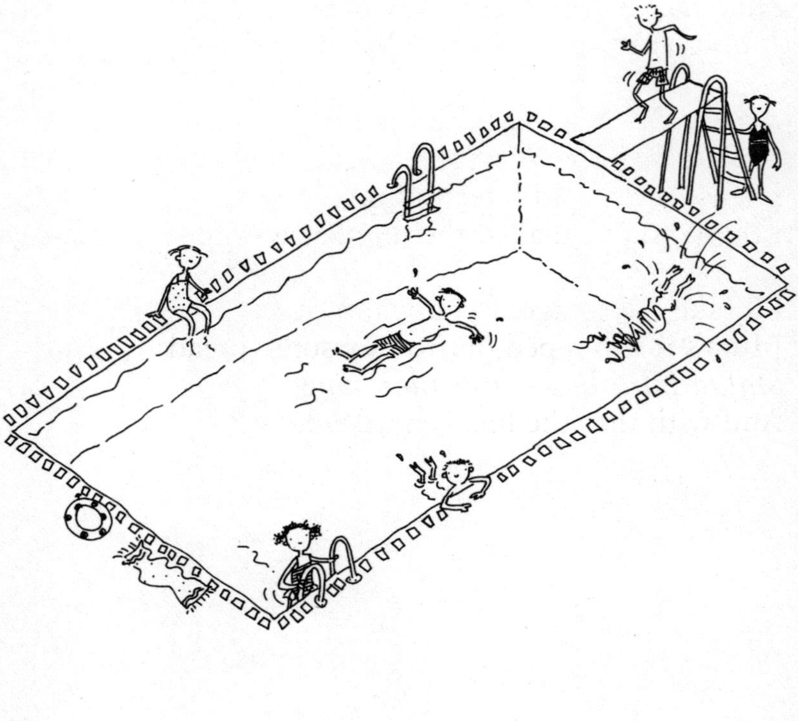

Message for Mum

Mum left her mobile phone in the kitchen
It rang and so I answered it
Hello, a buzzy voice enquired,
Star Commander – are you fit?

Battle cruisers in position?
Are the warheads timed and toggled?
Is the laser death-ray charged up?
Have the mind-warp bombs been boggled?

Across vast galaxies we've travelled
With our huge invasion fleet
Now we've found this puny planet
It doesn't look too hard to beat

Across the starfield's endless oceans
Will be heard our victory song . . .
Excuse me, I said interrupting,
I think you've dialled the number wrong

I'll take a message if you want
Mum's just popped out to buy some bread
Stupid Earthling – are you joking?
And with that the line went dead.

Julius Caesar's Last Breakfast

I'm tired this morning
Off my food
Hardly touched the olives, lark or dormouse
We stayed out late last night
With Lepidus
And talked of death
Drank too much wine
And now Calpurnia, my wife,
Is in a mood
She dreamed a death
And it was mine.

I'm tired this morning
The winds of March
Are blowing like a hurricane
Through Rome
At the Pontifical Palace
The God of Mars crashed to the floor
And what that means, I'm not quite sure.

I'm tired this morning
Upon the Ides of March
The Senate can convene without me
Yes, I think I'll stay at home.

(On the morning of Julius Caesar's assassination, the chamber at the Senate was full. But Caesar's chair was empty. He was nowhere to be found. The conspirators sent Marcus Brutus to Caesar's house to persuade him to attend.)

Egyptian Afterlife

So, Osiris, please tell me
What happens when I die?

First, mortal,
you must persuade the ferryman
to ferry you across
the river of death

And if I manage that?

Then you must pass through
The Twelve Gates
Each guarded
by a ferocious serpent

Twelve gates?
Sounds tricky.
But if I make it?

Your third ordeal will be to cross
The blazing Lake of Fire
Where you will be judged

Oh, I see. And if by chance
I've led a blameless life?

Why, you will live forever
And your soul
Will travel through
The heavens

But what if I have sinned?

Ha! Then you
will be fed to the monster!

Why bother with the journey?
Just feed me to the monster now.

The Knitting Club

Click click click click
Knit one, purl one
Knitting my nephew
a cardigan.

There goes another one.
Sneezing in the basket.
Wonder what it was he'd done?

Swwwiiissshhh
Oooooooooohhhh!
Clunk!
Plop!
Aaaaahhhhhhh!

This new guillotine
She's better than the old one.
The blade was getting rusty.
Didn't always cut clean.

Click click click click
What are you knitting, Anne-Marie?
Ah, mon amie, did you see that?
The executioner, he smiled at me.

Here comes today's last prisoner
Then we can all go home.

Swwwiiissshhh
Oooooooooohhhh!
Clunk!
Plop!
Aaaaahhhhhhh!

Time to get the supper on.

(At the time of the French Revolution, a group of women used to go to the executions at the guillotine and take their knitting with them to make a day of it. They were called The Knitting Club.)

Joan of Arc

Everyone thought it odd
that Joan of Arc heard voices

From God.

For being a witch and for foretelling that the
English would be defeated by the French and
thrown out of France (except for Calais), she was
burned at the stake which, in those less-civilized
and deadly times, is about what one might expect.
But as it turned out she was

Correct.

The Song of Winter

The Song of Winter
Is sung by the wind
With music so sad the trees share it
The words to the song
Are told by the wind
So sad that the heart cannot bear it

A Time to Heal
(haiku)

I hadn't seen her

For eleven silent years

I showed her my scar

A Time to Embrace

Mum hugged me
Said goodbye
And I climbed aboard the train

Dark clouds drifted overhead
And embraced the fields
With rain

A Time to Be Silent

Before the soccer game
In the stadium
We remembered the tragedy
When so many supporters died

For one minute
Fifty thousand
Men, women and children
Were silent

Even insects and birds
Seemed to sense
The moment
And were quiet

The wind held its breath
And time slowed

It was the loudest silence
I have ever heard.

The Estuary Field Trip

I walked with my class along the estuary
The salty wind sneaked through the cracked
  concrete
of time-worn sea defences,
stirred the weeds and rusty wire
that rose from the caked mud bed.
Thirty children poked under rocks
hunting for crabs
and tugged at a lump of driftwood,
perhaps once part of a sailing barge
taking bricks to London.

Isn't it beautiful? I said
Richard looking at me, nodded, smiled
A rare moment
A mystical union of teacher and pupil
Mr Stevens, said Richard,
Did you see the Man U game last night?

Don't Miss the Boat

The Woebegoing cried big fat tears
as the animals entered the Ark.
He'd been packing his case for thirteen years,
at first for a bit of a lark.
But now, as the animals boarded the ship,
he sat on the bank and bit his lip.

For thirteen years he'd searched the land
looking for a mate.
For thirteen years he'd sifted sand,
but now it was too late.
He rang his bell,

sung

a farewell song
and the Woebegoing
was the Woebegone.

Mr Walton's on the Playground

Michael's ball is on the roof
And Darren wants a fight
Little Kelly Kupcake
Is dangling from her kite

But Mr Walton's on the playground
So everything will be all right

Noel went in the girl's loo
And gave the girls a fright
Yaseen won't let Gemma kiss him
But Derek Trubsall might

But Mr Walton's on the playground
So everything will be all right

Randeep's lost his pet rat
(He *says* it doesn't bite)
Michael says – Aren't people small
When viewed from this great height?

But Mr Walton's on the playground
So everything will be all right

Tommy's foot is swelling up
His laces are too tight
Now Michael's stuck up on the roof.
He'll have to stay all night.

But Mr Walton's on the playground
So everything will be er...

Where's Mr Walton gone?

Birds at Play

We lined up after play
And Mrs Fudge shouted at Clint
Her breath like a smoky dragon
And we all trooped into the warm
But
I'd left my gloves on the wall
And so I ran back along the corridor
On to the playground
And stopped and stared
Amazed.

The playground
Was alive with birds
Eating dropped crisps and crumbs
And chasing and arguing and chattering
Starlings hopping amongst the gulls
And sparrows darting between the starlings
I hadn't realized
That the birds have a playtime
Immediately after ours.

Mysteries of the Universe

We went by coach
to the Planetarium
and witnessed the mysteries
of the Universe

We saw the birth of stars
black holes
comets trailing cosmic dust
and discussed
the existence of aliens

But a great mystery awaited us all

When we'd left school
sixty-two of us had boarded the coach

When we arrived back at school
sixty-three of us got off

The New Teacher

He tried to be funny.
He cracked a few jokes.
But he looked scared
To me.

He told us he was strict.
He did that long silence.
The *I Can Wait As Long As You* thing.
But when Des burped
He lost it – and shouted.

He's obviously quite bright.
He can rattle off his seven times table.
No problem.

He tells an interesting story.
It was a shame Fiona fidgeted.
And had to be sent to the Head Teacher's office.

I quite like him.
But I don't think he's up to it.
I can't see him staying the course.

A pity, really.

Teacher's Pet

Teacher's pet isn't Billy
or Darren or Sharon or Lee
Teacher's pet isn't Sally
or Vicky or Nicky or me
Teacher's hunting for her pet
She's crawling around on all fours
Teacher's pet is a big black spider
And she keeps it in her drawers.

Drum Kit for Sale

Drum Kit for Sale
Guaranteed to make house shake
Very Loud Indeed
(Gave Mum a headache.)

Drum Kit for Sale
Snappy snare – terrific tone
Dad says – *Must go at any price!*

(Or will exchange
for trombone.)

Corrections

Teacher said,
Leave out the the,
two too's one too too many
and and after the comma
should go after the any.

The the, the too –
and move the and
and that should make it flow.
Not that that, that that's fine –
but this that, that could go.

I said,
The the, the too, the and –
I would agree with you.
But I am very fond of that –
this that and that that too.

Which that is that?
Is that this that?
Asked teacher with a grin.
OK – but take that last in out
And leave that last out in.

The Supermarket for Lonely People

Walking along deserted aisles
you'll find
a solitary tin of smiles

Past the pet food
the smell of fresh-baked hugs
hangs in the air

On the shelves sit
bottled-up words of kindness
all wishing they'd been spoken

As you pass through the empty tills
the check-out person
makes you a special offer

Messages

At school
when I'm feeling low
I whisper a secret message into my hand
and hold it tightly in my fist
until playtime.
Then I release my message,
Watching it soar
like a carnival balloon
into the speckled sky.

At night, when Mum has turned out the light,
I think of Dad
and I'm sad that he's dead
but I still have the message
he whispered to me.
I pick up the conch shell
by my bed
and listen again.

I hear him,
like the echo of a shooting star
in the seas of space.
Don't worry, he whispers,
I love you.

Advice for Staging Your own Olympic Games

Never play volleyball with a bag of flour
Never use Mum's hairbrush as a baton in the relay
  race
The flower bed is not a sandpit for the long jump
And remember – the Olympic Games does not
  include kiss-chase

Never pole-vault in the vicinity of Grandpa's
  greenhouse
Never throw the discus using Mum's best plates
The broom handle is not a pole – nor is it a javelin
Never use flowerpots (especially if they have flowers
  in) for weights

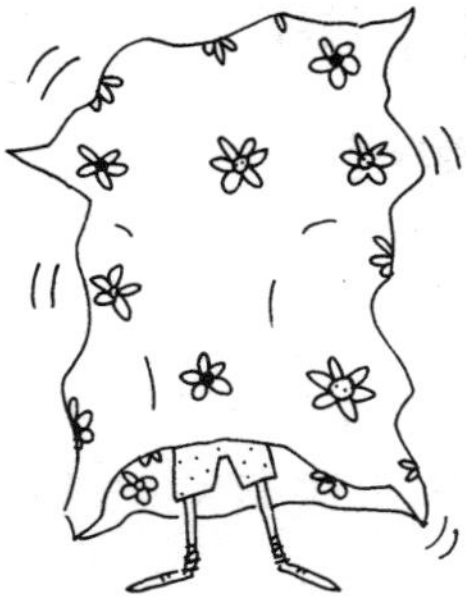

Your dog is a dog, not a horse
Although, at a push, could be used for equestrian
events
Do not use the duvet covers in the airing cupboard
To make those big marquee-type tents

Never use The Complete Set of Delia Smith for the
winners' podium
Never bribe the judges with crisps, chocolate,
football cards or cash.
And finally, when Mum comes home to find her
house and garden in a mess
Say, Excuse me, but I'm in the hundred metres –
must dash!

After School

After a stressful day at school

Don't you find

It's good to turn on the TV

And unwind

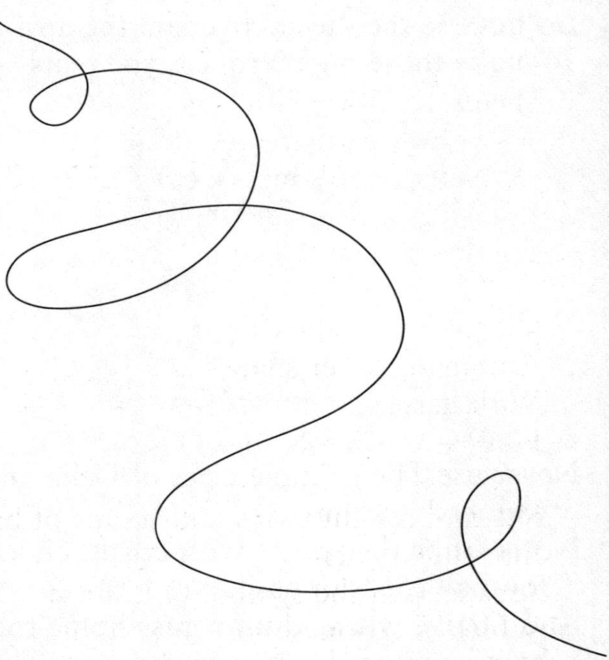

Cat Message

Shemu the cat
Whose ancestors
Prowled amongst the pyramids
Today received a special visitor

Neferhotep
Ambassador
From the constellation of Orion

Upon Neferhotep's
Departure
Shemu tried her best
To warn her mistress
Of Neferhotep's message

The Earth is about to be invaded

Shemu lay on the carpet
And made letter shapes
With her body
I – N – V – A – S – I – O – N

Shemu brought twigs and scraps of bark
Into the kitchen
Arranged in the symbol O-ki-hran
Which is Orionese for
You are about to be invaded by hideous aliens
From the constellation Andromeda

Shemu even reprogrammed the video
To play *Star Trek* tapes
But Shemu's only reward
For her efforts was some tinned cat-food

Humans, thought Shemu,
Can be so . . .
Dumb.

Mobile Home for Sale

Judy is a delightful
Mobile Home
with Central Heating
a warm Basement
Superb Penthouse Views
and includes luxury
Deep Pile Carpets
in black and white
Fully Air-Conditioned
by large wagging tail
This Border Collie
would suit large family of fleas.

Poems Written by Judy Dog...

A Dog's Dilemma

It might seem obvious to you humans
But it puzzles me every day
If he wants the stick so badly
Why does he throw it away?

Taking My Human for a Walk

I took my human for a walk along the beach
The fishing nets had dragged up
Hundreds of spider crabs
Dead and rotting on the shingle
I rolled and rolled in them
Sheer bliss

When we got home
I nearly died of embarrassment
My human said,
'Look, you have a crab's claw
stuck to your tail.'

Night Patrol

Before we settle down to sleep
It's my job to check the four corners
Of the garden

Behind the bins for lurking rats

Search the long shed shadows
Lest the Beast of Midnight is waiting there

Check the pond for late-night hoppers

Patrol the fence for creeping cats

All is well and I have a warm feeling
Knowing that my humans
Can sleep safely at night

Not to be outdone – Scampi cat wrote the following…

I Did Not Eat the Goldfish

I did not eat the goldfish
It was not me
At the time of the crime
I was sitting in a tree

I did not eat the goldfish
That's no word of a lie.
I loved his silvery fins
And his mischievous eye

I did not eat the goldfish
I did not touch one golden scale
And I've no idea why there's pondweed
Hanging from my tail

A Cat's Boundless Love

I love you, my mistress,
With a boundless love
That's bigger than the sky
And I bring you presents
To express my devotion

A worm
Caught in the early light of dawn,
Wet with dew and earth

Half a mouse
For you I save the delicacy
Of the beast's internal organs

A small fluttering bird
I save the pleasure of the creature's death
For you

Please
Do not betray me again

Missing Monty

Winter was coming
When Monty went missing
Oh, how I missed
His sibilant hissing

I searched high and low
I searched thin and long
Oh, where had my
Pet python gone?

Soon Christmas carols
Then Auld Lang Syne
Of missing Monty
There was no sign

Then just when I'd given him
Up for dead
On the first day of Spring
He turned up in my bed

Safe in my mattress
Tucked away out of sight
Just think, I'd been keeping
Him warm every night.

Visitor

Up close the gull was huge
Tapping angrily on the window
Of my bedroom.
I wondered, was it hungry?
It made loud sounds
Like an inarticulate window cleaner.
Did it want to come in?

It came back every half an hour or so.
I thought maybe it had adopted our house
As its territory

Until Mum popped her head out of the window
And saw its little, brown-grey baby,
With bright eyes and punky hair
Perched on the tiny ledge.

Farewell
(from *The Book of Gull*)

All whose flight makes lesser birds weep
Join with us in the Great Ocean Cry of Anguish

The cry that unlocks the black cloud
The cry that roils the smooth waters
The cry that drives all fish (save the shark
whose heart is ice) to the quaking depths

Join with us to say goodbye to our friend
Whose eye was as bright as sungleam
Whose voice cried with joy
Whose wing rode the wind's wild rhythms
Who danced in the wavespray
And soared high and free like a song

We will miss you

Wizard

In his white and yellow robes
The powerful and frightening
Wizened old wizard holds his magic wand
High in the stormy sky
And commands the mighty river,
Its white and foaming waters
Rolling huge rocks in its raging torrent,
To cease.
At once all is still.
And in that timeless
Silence
We cross the stepping stones
To the safety of the far bank.

Hurry up, Mum says, as we cross the road
Have you got your lunch box?

Shelley

I was thinking about my dog,
Shelley.
She died a while ago
but you still remember friends, don't you,
friends who have passed away.
She was unhappy at the end,
confused, she would bump into
the furniture and stand
staring into the corner of the room.
But I was thinking about the good times.
When she leapt into the icy water
at Betws-y-coed
and had to be rescued.
She loved swimming in the sea
and shaking herself dry over sunbathers,
especially old wrinkly ones.
She was a great one for fetching
sticks and balls –
you couldn't take her to tennis matches.
You know, sometimes I think I hear her
in the next room.
I forget she's gone.
Just the wind, I suppose,
rippling through my memories.

Longing for Wide Open Spaces

Do
You ever
Feel that the
World is closing in?
Asif thereis notime tothink
Asyouwalk alongthestreet
Peoplejostlingandpushing
And you want to shout
Givemesomeroomtobreath
Andyoudreamofclamberinghighhills
Climbingabovethecrowdsinthewideopencountryside
Just y o u

A l o n e   w i t h   t h e

F   o   r   e   v   e   r

s

k

y

Tightrope

Whilst walking the tightrope   try not to cough   in case you fall

o
f

f

Insult

A notion currently being inspected by
My brain is that
The glands beneath your skin
That produce minute particles
Designed to be carried
By tiny airborne currents
And picked up by nerves
In the mucous membrane
Covering the upper turbinal bone
And the nasal septum
Thus triggering impulses
Along olfactory nerves
Passing through minute holes
In the cribriform plate
Of the ethmoid bone
Into the olfactory bulb
In the nose
And so to the
Olfactory tract
In the brain
Are over-producing
Again

Or to put it
Another way –

I think
You stink!

Night Puzzle

going round and round my head and why did you say those words you said and how can I sleep with those words

The Winning Goal

When I scored the winning goal
I had never felt so alone
The crowd went crazy, on their feet
But my heart sank like a stone
They say that scoring is marvellous,
The best feeling that's ever been known,
But it's hard to take
When you make a mistake
And the back of the net
is your own.

Michael Owen

Michael Owen, Michael Owen

Runs so fast his boots are glowing

Kicks the ball for all he's worth

Now it's orbiting the Earth

The World's Greatest Goalie

I fly down the wing
Make a thunderous shot
Score a fabulous goal
That's the tenth I've got
I love my mum
I love her a lot
Is she a great goalie?
I'm afraid she's not.

Regrets

From where I sit
the roar of the crowd
is like distant thunder
shaking the ground

It's lonely here
away from the fun,
the long pass, the short ball,
the cannon-fire shot
shaking the goal

Sitting here all alone
in the silent dressing room
with the ghosts of great players
is hard
I didn't mean to hit him
I lost my temper
and saw red –
the referee's red card.

They Don't Know Everything

My mum and stepdad
Know everything
Or so they think
But

Only I know
The routes of alien spaceships
Criss-crossing the night sky

Only I know
The hidden art of invisibility
And how to fly

Only I know
The password to the hidden door
Behind the rakes in the garden shed

Only I know the secret tongue of lizards
And why the dragons
Are all dead

I'll never tell my folks what I have found
And when I'm grown-up I'll keep these secrets
Safe and sound.

Mum & Dad

Tenderskin & Roughchin
Dawngreeter & Toastjuggler
Cuddlebear & Grizzlybear
Firmhand & Strongarm
Sadsmile & Grinner
Busybee & Grasshopper
Spicegrinder & Potstirrer
Sunsoaker & Ballspinner
Spidershrieker & Jarcatcher
Taleteller & Dreamweaver
Earthmother & Earthmover

Pencil Incident

When I was seven
I pushed a pencil through
The arm of the armchair
From one side to the other.
After Dad had told me off he said,
'We'll draw a line
under this incident, shall we?'

I said,
'Shall we use my pencil?'
That was a mistake.

Walking the Dog Seems Like Fun to Me

Dad said, The dog wants a walk.

Mum said to Dad, It's your turn.
Dad said, I always walk the dog.
Mum said, Well I walked her this morning.
Dad said, She's your dog –
I didn't want a dog in the first place.

Mum said, It's your turn.

Dad stood and threw the remote control
at the pot plant.
Dad said, I'm going down the pub.
Mum said, Take the dog.

Dad shouted, No way!
Mum shouted, You're going nowhere!

I grabbed Judy's lead
and we both bolted out the back door.

The stars were shining like diamonds.
Judy sniffed at a hedgehog, rolled up in a ball.
She ate a discarded kebab on the pavement.
She chased a cat up a tree.

Walking the dog
seems like fun to me.

My Thin Friend

Here lies the body

Of stick-insect Fred

He didn't move for three whole days

I hope he *was* dead

Lowku Haiku

If a poem has

Just sixteen syllables

Is it a lowku?

Phobia Attack

I was in bed
Thinking I really must get up
When my sister screamed
from the bathroom
'Quick! Quick!
A spider!'
I grabbed a glass
And a piece of card
'Hurry! It's the biggest
spider you ever saw!'
I dashed along the passage
To the bathroom . . .

Too late!
My sister had gone
The phobia had eaten her

Prayer for Worms Everywhere

Dear God
Who each day blesses
The early bird
Today
Please bless
The worm

Plenty More Pebbles on the Beach

Rock, split by rain
And ocean spray,
Falls into ocean

Surf wanderers
Sea skimmers
Tide tumblers
Slate skaters
Smooth talkers
Shell splitters
Crab crushers
Wave chasers

Into the future
Finely ground to sand

James Bond's Car

So this, you say, was James Bond's car
Did you get it from a dealer?
I love the feel of the steering wheel.
Don't touch that lever!

I love the colour – the go-faster stripes
The upholstery of leather
And nozzle for making oil skids.
Don't touch that lever!

An in-board computer with gadgets galore
Pours lemonade – if you need a breather –
And is this a rocket launcher? Wow!
Don't touch that lever!

I wish I had a James Bond car.
It's a real scene-stealer.
And look – it's got ejector seats.

Don't touch that . . .
AAAAAAaaaaaaaaaaaaaaaaaaaaahhhhhhhh

My Stepdad is an Alien

I'd suspected for some time.
I finally got up the courage
to talk to him about it.

I think you're an alien, I told him.

Nonsense, he said. Why do you think that?

You're bald. You don't have any hair
anywhere.

That's not that unusual, he said.

Well, you've got one green eye
and one blue one.

That doesn't make me an alien, he replied.

You can make the toaster work
without turning it on.

That's just a trick, he smiled.

Sometimes I hear you
talking to Mum in a weird alien language.

I'm learning Greek
and Mum lets me practise on her.

What about your bright blue tail?

Ah, he said thoughtfully.
You're right, of course.
So, the tail gave it away, did it?

I'll Miss My Gran

My gran's going to die soon.
Mum told me last night,
I suppose it had to happen one day.
I suppose I hadn't thought about it much.

I'll miss her funny stories
about the good old days.

Mum says
we all die sooner or later.
The thing to do
is to have a good time when you're young,
to build up your memory bank
for when you're old.
Then you'll have lots of funny stories
to tell your own grandchildren.

Well, for Mum that might be OK
but I'm not having grandchildren.

No way!

My Dad

My Dad's a cobbler
He mends shoes
He's my cobbling Dad

He dropped the hammer on his toe
He's my hobbling, cobbling Dad

Dad had an argument with a customer
He's my squabbling, hobbling, cobbling Dad

So he made her a raspberry jelly
He's my wobbling, squabbling, hobbling, cobbling
  Dad

Then he ate it all himself
He's my gobbling, wobbling, squabbling, hobbling,
  cobbling Dad

Werewolf Granny

When midnight chimes
And the moon is full
And the wind is whistling
Down the hall
When you hear the hoot
Of frightened owls
The werewolf granny prowls

By the light of day
You would never guess
That our dear old granny
In her woolly vest
Sipping her tea
And humming a tune
Will be out in the park
When the night grows dark
Howling at the moon

When midnight chimes
And the moon is full
And the wind is whistling
Down the hall
Lock your door
When you go to bed
Pull the duvet
Over your head
When you hear the hoot
Of frightened owls
The werewolf granny prowls

So be good to your granny
And always say please
Give her a hug,
A kiss and a squeeze
For it might be a rumour
But it just might be true
That one dark, dismal night
When the full moon's bright
She will be after you

The End of the World

Uncle Bill
Foretold the future
The future from him
Wasn't hid
One day he predicted
The world would end
And for him
It did

LOUDER!

OK, Andrew, nice and clearly – off you go.

Welcome everybody to our school concert ...

Louder, please, Andrew. Mums and dads won't hear you at the back, will they?

Welcome everybody to our school concert ...

Louder, Andrew. You're not trying.
Pro – ject – your – voice.
Take a b i g b r e a t h and louder!

Welcome everybody to our school concert ...

For goodness sake, Andrew. LOUDER! LOUDER!

Welcome ev
erybody to our
school conc
ert!

Now, Andrew, there's no need to be silly.

Never Trust a Lemon

Never trust a lemon
It's a melon in disguise
Never trust potatoes
With shifty eyes
Never trust a radish
It repeats all that it hears
Never trust an onion
It will all end in tears

The Last Day of My Holiday
(a Haiku poem)

When we left Grove Park
My best mate went to one school
I went somewhere else

We arranged to meet
To play tennis in the park
I was kitted-out

He lived across town
It was a long, hot bike ride
It would be worth it

I knocked on his door
He's at school, his mum told me
They went back today

As I cycled home
My head buzzed like a bees' nest
My eyes were stinging

He was my best friend
How could he do that to me?
Just a joke, he said.

Where Do Poems Come From?

I found an idea for a poem
Down the back of the sofa.
It was just out of reach,
Which was annoying,
And I had to reach down
Behind the cushions,
Right up to my elbow,
To fetch it out.

I also found a pound coin.

Treasure Trail

Normally
I get home from school
and go straight out again
to the park
but today

I spotted a penny on the hall floor
and as I bent to pick it up
I spotted another –
one pace away.

As I bent to pick that up
I spotted another –
one pace away.

As I bent to pick that up
I spotted yet another
on the bottom step
of the stairs.

I picked it up
and spied another
on the third step

and another on the seventh
and another on the tenth
and another at the top.

At the top of the stairs
I spotted a five pee
on the landing –
one pace away.

At this rate I was going to be rich.
I followed the trail
to the door of my room.

The door was open
and I could see
a ten pee
on my floor.

I went in, and,
as I bent to pick it up,
the door slammed shut
behind me.

I tried to open it
but it was shut fast.
A note was pinned to the door.

It said, You are my prisoner.
You are not getting out
until you have tidied your room!
Signed
Mum

And all for
twenty-three pee!

lower case poet

e.e.cummings
was an american poet
who never used
capital letters
he, also, liked:
to-ex-per-i:me-nt:
w/i/t/h/
irregu;
larpunc;
tuation;
I tried this once in (english)
and I don't thin (k
the teacher)
reallyappreciatedmy(ef)
forts

The Idea Hunt

I've got to write a poem
I've got to write it here
I'm running out of time
But I've got no idea

And an idea's what I need.
What can I write about?
I had some ideas yesterday
But the ideas all ran out.

I chased after the ideas
And pleaded, Please come back!
They turned around and laughed and said,
You won't catch us like that.

Where do ideas come from?
I've been hunting them for ages
Under stones and gooseberry bushes
And in the Yellow Pages.

I've got to write a poem
What am I going to do?
I can't think of a poem.
I haven't got a clue.

So I went to my teacher
And told her of my plight
She said, But you've just written one.
And I said, Gosh, you're right.